West Coast Wild

Big Fish Little Fish
Fish Tales & Recipes

Copyright © 2017 Jackie Elliott All rights reserved

Originally Published December 2014

Revised Edition Published December 2017

Language: English

Photography:

Cassandra Jean Photography

Jessica Breeze Photography

Matt & Melissa Photography

Jason Elliott

With Thanks to the Elliott Family for recipes & family photographs.

ISBN# 978-0-9939542-1-4

Contents

Introduction 1

Memories of Elliott's Point 4

Salmon Marinade 6

Ray's Stuffed Salmon 8

Smoked Salmon 11

My First Cooking Job 13

Smoked Salmon Pate 16

Smoked Salmon Tartlets 17

Canning Salmon 19

Salmon & Caper Fish Cakes 21

Pickled Salmon 23

Halibut Ceviche 27

Halibut Filo Parcels 28

Halibut Cheeks Asiago 30

Chipotle Seafood Bake 31

Mason Jar Fish Pie 32

Fish Tacos 33

The Skeeter II 36

Coquilles St. Bob 37

A Family Fishing Affair 39

Norm's Seafood in a Bun 40

Crab Cakes 42

Spicy Tomato Relish 43

Layered Crab Dip 45

Mushroom Seafood Caps 47

Prawn Fishing with Uncle Muck 50

Grilled Prawns 51

Prawn Cocktail 53

Prawn Risotto 54

Prawn Curry 56

Mussels in White Wine & Garlic 59

Broiled Ginger Scallops 60

Pan Seared Scallops with Mint Pesto 61

Digging Clams 63

Clam Fritters 64

Seafood Chowder 66

Bannock 67

Seafood Salad 68

Seafood & Black Bean Pasta 69

Pan Fried Oysters 71

Smoked & Canned Oysters 72

The Silver Eagle 74

Introduction

I fell in love with my future husband when he cooked halibut cheeks for me. Until that evening, I had no idea that halibut even had cheeks.

But I was really glad they did, because after I ate that meal, I could have died right then and it would have been OK. But I didn't, I went on to marry Bob Elliott, who continues to cook for me, and it seemed madness that we didn't capture every recipe and help make people the world over as happy as me when I am eating seafood.

So this project was born.

The majority of these recipes are seafood and call for fresh seafood. If you are not as lucky as us to have access to plentiful wild seafood, don't despair, it is still possible to enjoy these recipes.

When buying seafood, purchase as close to the source as possible. If you can't buy straight from commercial fishermen at the dock, find a local reputable fishmonger or fish market, and ask the vendors for daily recommendations.

If you have no alternative but your local supermarket, buy from the seafood counter, but ask to smell the fish before you buy - if it smells fishy - don't buy it, it's not fresh.

Cook the fish as soon as possible after purchasing it.

Except where stated, the recipes and stories come from Bob, my only task was to write everything down and arrange it. Oh, and to test every recipe of course. It was a tough job but I muddled through!

My thanks goes to the Elliott family for sharing photos and recipes. I hope I have correctly credited you all with the origin of these recipes.

We hope you enjoy cooking these recipes.

We are always open for new ideas, so if you have an idea to improve on a recipe, or if you have questions or comments, please contact me at jackie.elliott@shaw.ca

Happy Cooking!

Jackie Elliott

On the East Coast of Vancouver Island, about half an hour's drive from the small coal town of Ladysmith, you will find Elliott's Park Beach, or Elliott's Point, as my family refer to it.

It's a shallow sloping bay, distinguished by a large Maple tree, which bows down at the main curve of the beach.

During high tide, kids can hurl themselves into the water from the rope attached to the main branch, and parents can find shade from the summer sun.

Back at the turn of the century, Norman Elliott, my grandfather, owned Elliott's farm, about 100 acres on Yellow Point, beside Klueet Bay Indian Reserve.

In the 1960's, the farm was sold, but Norman Ellott retained the rights to a public access to Elliott's Point so he could launch his boat.

If you look at any picture album in my family, you will find photos of generations of us at Elliott's Point, from the time that cameras were invented to the present day.

We've celebrated birthday's and weddings, enjoyed summer picnics, we fished, swam and built camp fires on this beach. We said our goodbyes to loved ones here too.

Food was an important part of all these family gatherings. Fresh fish cooked on an open fire, clams, and crab - everything the ocean had to offer.

Watching the elders cook when I was a kid at Elliott's Point, ere my first cooking lessons. Now that I'm an elder, I am ready to share all that I know about seafood and cooking.

I hope you enjoy these recipes and share them with your family.

Bob Elliott

Salmon Marinade

During the summer months at Elliott's Point, we ate barbequed salmon cooked the traditional native way, help by "sticks" over an open fire (see cover photo).

Dad (Ray Elliott) started the tradition of marinating the fresh salmon before cooking it. He used soy sauce and garlic. over the years, the recipe developed and just about everyone in the family has their own version - claiming to be the "secret" Elliott's Point recipe.

This is my version.

Ingredients

2 Cups Soy Sauce

1/2 Cup Teriyaki Marinade 1 Cup Brown Sugar

1/2 Cup Dijon Mustard 1/4 Cup Olive Oil

1 orange, sliced (peel on) Juice of 1 lemon

Small chunk of ginger root, diced 1 tsp Garlic Powder.

Mix all the ingredients together in a large bowl.

Place fresh (not frozen) salmon fillets in the mixture and allow to marinate in the fridge overnight, or as long as possible.

Take the fillets out, drain off excess liquid and cook immediately on a hot grill or BBQ.

Ray's Stuffed Salmon

My Dad, Ray "bear" Elliott was a logger and a fisherman. he was also a great cook. This is one of his recipes, and traditionally, if you are a fisherman, this is the way the first sockeye salmon of the season is prepared on the boat.

Ingredients

1 large fresh salmon (head on)

1 loaf of bread, broken into 1/2 inch cubes

1/2 lb butter, melted

3 large onions, chopped

4 tbsps of poultry seasoning

1 lemon, sliced (peel on)

Juice of 2 lemons

Salt and pepper to taste

Combine all the ingredients in a large bowl, except the sliced lemon, and mash up thoroughly (easier to use your hands).

Clean the salmon inside, making sure that there are no guts or blood left in the cavity. Salt the fish inside.

Place the cleaned and salted salmon on a large piece of aluminum foil - large enough to wrap the whole fish.

Stuff the bread mixture into the fish's cavity. Shove in as much as possible - even if it is spilling out.

Place the slices of lemon on top of the fish, and then wrap the whole salmon in the foil

Bake in an oven at 350 degrees for an hour or longer depending on the size of the fish

Smoked Salmon

Fishing season is only a few weeks in the summer, so to preserve a stock of fish for the winter, West Coast First Nations (my ancestors) would smoke fish. It was also useful to barter with other tribes for wild game.

My grandmother used to hang sides of salmon over an open fire in a large smoke house for up to 10 days until they were as stiff as boards. The only seasoning she used was salt. Fish smoked this way can keep for months. It can be eaten by tearing strips and chewing it like jerky, or it can be re-hydrated in boiled water.

These days, smoking salmon is more of a delicacy than a preserving method. Fishermen can take their catch to commercial smoke houses, or smoke their own fish.

I smoke mine in a smoke house I built from plywood - but you can purchase small "smokers" which will take small quantities of fish. The key is to keep the temperature down around 120 degrees, and make sure the smoke house or smoker is well ventilated. Otherwise, the fish ends up baked rather than smoked.

The choice of wood will affect the flavour, I prefer maple or alder.

To prepare the fish, clean and fillet. Using the salmon marinade recipe, brush each fillet and leave overnight in the fridge.

The next morning, build the fire so it is smoking well, and the smoker or smoke house is starting to heat up.

Smoked Salmon *(cont)*

Sprinkle the marinated fillets with soft brown sugar, and place in the smoke house.

Smoke the fish for approx 6 hours, if you are using a smoke house, about 3 or 4 hours if using a small smoker.

Check the fire / temperature regularly. If the fillets get too hot, you will see white fat appearing on the surface of the fish. This means that the natural oils are being lost, which will affect the flavour.

After the fish has been smoking for a while, a "crust" will start to appear on the surface. At this point, I like to brush the fillets with liquid honey and continue smoking for approximately 4 more hours. This give the sweet and salty flavour referred to as "Indian Candy".

In the picture below you can see the deep intense colour of the smoked fish when it is ready.

My favourite way to eat smoked salmon is straight out of the smoke house, but it is excellent with crackers and cream cheese, or with salads.

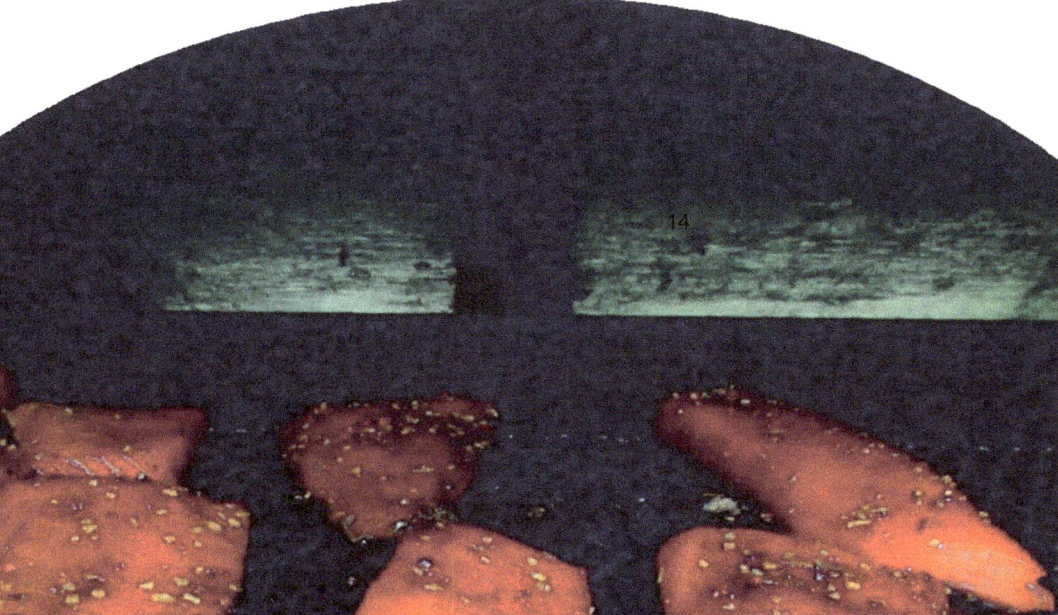

My First Cooking Job

I was sixteen, and had my first fishing job on "The Searcher". I was skiff man, which meant I was the lowest form of life. My job was to row the beach man to the beach, work on deck, and do everything that no one else wanted to do.

It was a humiliating experience.

However, my career was fast tracked when the cook quit. It was a thankless job, so I got it. Only problem was... I had no idea how to cook.

First meal I got to prepare was pancakes for breakfast. Easy right? No, I had only a small amount of pancake mix left, so I just added a pile of flour and an extra egg. I had no clue about baking powder and all that stuff, so consequently the pancakes came out like small Frisbees.

And that's exactly what they were used for. The rest of the crew had a competition to see how far they could hurl my pancakes. The seagulls were excited at first, but even those scavengers couldn't gag down my first breakfast.

I took lessons in basic cooking. I sat in on evening classes, and instead of taking my western novels fishing, I took cookbooks. I learned more about spices and seasoning, and baking and eventually I wasn't a bad cook.

One thing that took a long time to get used to, was the quantity I was supposed to cook. My family is large - I am one of six kids, so my mum had to juggle with a limited budget to feed us all.

On the boat, I had an unlimited budget. I got to buy the very best cuts of meat, and the best ingredients, and it didn't matter how much it cost, I just had to make sure that I fed the crew the best food possible, but I still miscalculated on occasion.

One time, I had roasted a large chicken. One of the crew, an ex- wrestler, came in to dinner, stabbed the chicken with his fork, and ate the whole thing....I was in trouble for that.....

To this day I always make too much food, I never want to run out. And I always love to cook with the best, freshest meat, fish and produce I can find..... same as when I was fishing.

Smoked Salmon Paté

Smoked Salmon Paté

Ingredients

1 cup of diced smoked salmon

1/4 cup of butter, melted

1/4 cup of cream cheese

Juice of 1/2 lemon

Salt and pepper to taste.

Place smoked salmon, melted butter and lemon juice in a blender, and blend until smooth.

Add the cream cheese gradually, and blend until the desired consistency is reached.

Season to taste.

Serve with warm French bread for an appetizer or lunch.

Smoked Salmon Tartlets

Ingredients

20 individual savoury pie crusts (available in most supermarkets)

1 cup of diced smoked salmon 2 large eggs

1/z cups of sour cream 1/2 cup of cream cheese Salt and pepper to taste Pinch of cayenne pepper.

"Blind' bake the pie crusts for 10 mins in a hot oven, around 350 degrees. Leave the oven on. Let them cool, and then arrange the diced smoked salmon evenly in the 20 pie crusts.

In a bowl, beat the eggs, cream and cream cheese together with the seasoning. Spoon the mixture into the pie crusts, over the smoked salmon.

Sprinkle a pinch of cayenne pepper on each pie.

Bake in the hot oven for 25 mins, or until the tartlets are golden brown.

Purse Seining

Canning Salmon

Those early days fishing on "The Searcher" I occasionally got a couple of days off. The only problem was, my skipper, Lloyd Baynes liked to tie the boat up on Galiano Island, just off the East Coast of Vancouver Island.

So to get home, I had to row to Saltspring Island, hitchhike or walk to the ferry terminal, catch the ferry to Vancouver Island and then get a bus to Cedar.

One time, I had about 20 salmon to take home to mom. I stuffed them into a duffel bag with as much ice as I could shove in, and made the long trek from Galiano.

It all went well until I caught the bus at Crofton, about half an hour's ride to Cedar. The bus driver was grumpy, and at first wouldn't drop me off at Cedar - he was going all the way to Nanaimo.

However, it had been a warm day, so the ice was beginning to melt, and water and fish slime was starting to drip out of the duffel bag.

He practically threw me off the bus, exactly where I wanted to be... When I arrive home, mom and I immediately starting cutting up the fish, and we canned all day long, just in time for me to get back on the bus and head back to the boat for another trip.

To prepare salmon for canning, clean the fish thoroughly, and cut into steaks, trimming the fish so it will fit into 1 lb cans, or mason jars.

Canning Salmon *(cont)*

If you are using jars, they should be sterilized. NEVER re-use lids. The secret to successful canning is making being vigilant about sanitizing.

Once the fish is cut up, place in the cans or jars. Add half a teaspoon of sea salt.

Thoroughly wipe the rims of the cans or jar, before you place the lids on. If you are using cans, then the canner will seal the lids to the cans. It is possible to get either a hand cranked canner, or electric canner.

If using jars, make sure that the lids are screwed on tightly. The heat from the canning process will seal the lids.

Place the cans or jars into a large pressure cooker, with enough water to cover the first layer of cans.

Put the lid on, bring up to 10 lbs of pressure and then let it "cook" for ninety minutes, checking that the pressure does not go below 10 lbs.

Let the jars or cans cool, and then take them out, checking that each one has sealed, or maintained the seal. If there is ANY doubt, or if any of the jars have cracked , dispose of the unsealed containers or cracked jars immediately. The canned salmon will last for a few years - usually getting better with time!

Salmon & Caper Fish Cakes

Ingredients

2 cans of salmon

1 cups of mash potatoes - blend until smooth

1/2 cup of cream cheese

2 tbsps of drained and chopped capers 1 tbsp of lemon juice

1/2 tsp of cayenne pepper Salt and pepper to taste.

For the coating and frying 1 egg - beaten

1/2 cup of panko seasoned to your taste

1/z cup of canola and tbsp of butter.

Combine thoroughly all the ingredients for the fish cakes in a large bowl. Put the bowl into the fridge for a couple of hours to chill and firm.

Form the mixture into small patties of the same size, and arrange on a greased cookie sheet. Put into the freezer for an hour, until they are semi - hard.

(At this stage you can just take out the amount of patties you want to cook, leaving the rest to freeze completely - then take them off the cookie sheet and continue to store in the freezer in zip lock bag)

Dip each patty into the beaten egg and then coat with the panko mix.

Heat up canola oil with a little butter in a frying pan, and pan fry the patties until golden brown each side.

Pickled Salmon

This is a delicious way to preserve and enjoy salmon. This recipe is far less "fishy" than pickled herring.

My sister Debra provided the recipe for the pickled fish. Debra is a great chef, and has cooked in fishing lodges and local pubs.

Pickling fish is a multi-step process starting with salting down the fish for at least ten days.

For the Salting process

5 lbs of cleaned, skinned and filleted salmon - chum salmon works best

Large bag of coarse salt.

Cover the fillet of fish with salt - put salt in between the fillets with a large layer on top. Keep in a cool place, preferably a fridge. Leave for at least ten days.

When the fish is uncovered and the salt is brushed off, it should be a stiff as a board.

At the point, when the fish is easy to handle, cut into small bite size chunks.

Place all the chunks of fish into a large cooler, and run water off them to wash out the last of the salt. This process should last about 4 hours.

Pickled Salmon *(cont)*

Place all the chunks of fish into a large cooler, and run water off them to wash out the last of the salt. This process should last about 4 hours.

Mix around the chunks regularly and test the water for saltiness. When you cannot taste the salt any longer, the fish is ready for pickling.

For the Pickling Brine

6 cups of water

8 cups of pickling vinegar

2 cups of sugar

3 1/2 cups of pickling spices

Bring the ingredients to a boil in a large stock pot, and then simmer for 20 minutes. Cool thoroughly - overnight is best. Then strain the mixture, but retain the pickling spices.

You can pickle the salmon on its own or add onions. I use sweet white walla walla onions from Washington.

Once you have your rinsed salmon, cold pickling brine and chopped onions (if using) you are ready to jar the pickled fish.

I use quart jars. Sterilize the jars before use. Fill the jars with layers of onion and salmon pieces.

Make sure you don't pack them too tightly because it is important that the pickling brine surrounds all the fish, making sure it is cured properly.

Once the jars are full, add the pickling brine using a jug, fill to the brim of each jar, and tap them gently to release any air pockets.

Before you screw the lids on the filled jar, add a teaspoon of the retained pickling spice.

Store the jars in a cool space for about a week before opening and enjoying.

Halibut Ceviche Salad

"Ceviche" is typically a South American dish of raw fish marinated in citrus juices. Tuna and prawns are flavourful this way, this is my son Jason's halibut recipe.

Ingredients

3 lbs Halibut, thinly sliced

Juice of 8 limes

2 mangos.

1 red onion

1 cucumber

2 large tomatoes

2 orange or yellow bell peppers

2 hot peppers, jalapenos or serrano

Bunch of fresh cilantro.

Soak the slices of halibut in the lime juice overnight in the fridge. The next day, squeeze the juice out the halibut slices, and then mince it up.

Chop all the veg and fruit finely and add to the minced halibut. Chop the fresh cilantro and add to the mixture, and combine well. Serve chilled with crackers, as a side dish, or just scoop up delicious spoonfuls.

Halibut Filo Parcels

Ingredients

1 medium Halibut fillet - sliced so it is 3/4 inch thick

6 -10 sheet of filo pastry (depending on the size of your fillet, you want to have enough pastry to wrap the fillet at least 4 times)

1/4 cup of cream cheese 2 lb peeled prawns (optional)

1 tsp of dried dill

1 cup of melted butter.

Salt and pepper to season.

Season the halibut fillet(s). Grease a large cookie tray.

Lay the sheets of filo pastry on the cookie sheet, brushing each one liberally with melted butter, so they don't dry and crack,. Overlap them - the idea is to wrap the halibut fillets in a parcel of filo pastry.

Once you have all the filo pastry buttered and in place, put the halibut fillet(s) on top of the pastry, in the middle. Do not stack the fillets, or they will not cook property.

Smear the fillets with cream cheese, add the fresh prawns on top (if using), and sprinkle with the dill.

Wrap the fillets up with the filo pastry. Stick the flaps of pastry together with melted cheese. You should end up with a "halibut parcel".

Brush one more time with the butter over the top and sides, and bake in a pre-heated oven at medium heat for about half an hour, or until the filo pastry is brown and crunchy.

Let the parcel rest of a minute or two, and then slice into portions for a main meal, or into small bites as appetizers.

Halibut Cheeks Asiago

Halibut do have cheeks. They are the most delicate part of the fish. They look like large scallops, and just pan fried with the minimum seasoning, they will cut like butter, and melt in your mouth.

This recipe just takes it up a notch.

Ingredients

10 halibut cheeks

2 egg yolks, beaten

1 cup of seasoned all purpose flour 1 cup of panko

1 cup of asiago cheese, grated.

Canola oil for frying.

Mix the panko with the grated cheese.

Coat each cheek with the seasoned flour, shaking off the excess.

Then dip the cheeks first into the egg yolk mixture and then into the panko and cheese. Each cheek should be evenly coated.

Heat the canola oil in a shallow frying pan, and fry the cheeks on both sides until golden brown.

Serve immediately.

Chipotle Seafood Bake

Ingredients

1 lb of fresh halibut, diced in bite size cubes

1 lb of prawn tails, peeled

1 1/2 cups of cooked basmati rice 1 onion chopped finely

1 quart of sour cream

1 small can of chipotle peppers in sauce

1 cup of grated cheddar cheese.

In a food processor blend the sour cream with the can of chipotle peppers. Add the peppers gradually, and taste as you go, until you reach the taste and heat that you like.

Line a shallow casserole dish with the cooked rice.

In a frying pan, sear the halibut chunks on each side for 1 minute. Arrange the halibut chunks, and prawns over the layer of cooked rice. Over the seafood, pour the sour cream and chipotle mixture and smooth out so all the seafood is covered.

Sprinkle the cheddar cheese evenly over the whole dish.

Bake in a medium heat oven for approx. 25 minutes or until the cheese is bubbling and turning brown.

Mason Jar Fish Pie

Ingredients

1 lb halibut or cod (diced) 1/2 lb cooked shrimp

1 medium onion, finely chopped 2 medium carrots, finely chopped

5 large potatoes, cooked and mashed 2 tbps of sour cream

2 tbsp of butter 2 tbps of olive oil

1/2 cup of white wine

1/2 cup of ground parmesan cheese 1 cup of light cream

Tsp of dried dill

1 cup of seasoned all purpose flour.

Fry the carrots and onion in the olive oil in a large frying pan, until soft. Dip the diced halibut or cod in the seasoned flour and add to the frying pan. Saute for 2 minutes and then deglaze the frying pan with the white wine. Simmer for a couple of minutes and then add the light cream and stir until thickened.

In a blender, add the mashed potatoes, sour cream and butter and blend until smooth.

Add the cooked shrimp and dill to the seafood mixture in the frying pan, and stir and simmer for another minute.

Divide the seafood mixture evenly to six small wide mouth mason jars. Top with the potato mixture, sprinkle with parmesan cheese and bake in the oven at 350 degrees for 20 minutes or until the topping is golden brown.

Fish Tacos

Ingredients

1 packet tacos - soft or hard

1 lb of cod cubed Seasoning.

Canola oil / butter for frying

For the topping/ filling- all optional

Shredded lettuce

Grated Cheese

Chipotle Sour cream (blend a chipotle pepper with sour cream)

Avocado Salsa

1 ripe firm avocado 2 large ripe tomatoes

½ small red onion

1 tablespoon of chopped cilantro 2 tablespoons of fresh lime juice Few drops of tabasco sauce

Salt and pepper to taste

Chop avocado, tomatoes and onions into small chunks of similar size. Combine together in a bowl, add lime juice, cilantro and tabasco, cover with cling film and leave in fridge to allow flavours to develop.

Fry the seasoned cod cubes in canola oil and butter, until seared evenly and cooked through.

To make up a taco, take a shell, fill with a few cubes of pan fried cod, fill with your favourite toppings and dressing, and enjoy.

The Skeeter II

The first commercial fishing boat I ever owned was the Skeeter II. I bought it from Albert Fair (the builder) in 1977, when I was nineteen years old. In that boat, I fished halibut, prawns, salmon and packed herring.

I had very little equipment (just a sounder) and less experience - no clue at all what I was doing.

I eventually had to sell the Skeeter II in 1981, after I got stiffed by a fish buyer named "Dave" who bounced a check for $56,000 for a boat load of prawns. In those days it was a fortune, and the loss cost me my first boat.

I went on to run other boats, and later became joint owner of The Waverley, and then finally my pride and joy, The Silver Eagle.

But it was those first years that I learned the most about fishing....and more about business.

Coquilles St. Bob

Ingredients

1/2 lb each of scallops, shrimp and prawns

1/2 cup of white wine 1/4 cup of water

3 tbsp of butter

3 shallots, chopped

1 tsp salt

1 1/2 cups of light cream 2 tbsp of chopped parsley. 3 cups of creamy mashed potatoes

Handful of shredded parmesan and asiago cheese.

Combine the water, wine and shallots in a large saucepan and bring to the boil. Reduce the heat and add seafood. Simmer for five minutes.

Lift out the seafood.

Reduce the remaining liquid to 1/4 cup, add the butter and light cream and season with the salt. Add back the seafood and parsley and blend well.

Spoon into a baking dish and pipe the mashed potato mixture around the edge.

Sprinkle the cheese all over, and brown under a grill until the cheese bubbles.

A Family Fishing Affair

My boys, Norman and Jason came on the boat with me during the summer when I was fishing. They had to work, but looking back I think I made it fun too. Both of them still love to fish, and they are both awesome cooks too.

Sometimes, when I have given them my favourite recipes, they have adopted the recipe as if it were their own (see Norm's Seafood in a Bun).

In one picture you can see the boys holding (and wearing) Dungeness Crab. I caught these when I was diving in the Alberni Inlet, the centre of Vancouver Island.

We cooked these crab the old fashioned way.

I gave them a firm tap. I heated up rocks on the beach over a camp fire. I dug a hole and half filled it with seaweed. I rolled the rocks into the hole on top of the seaweed. The crabs went in after this, shell downwards, then I buried the crabs with seaweed. A stove on the beach! One hour later we had fresh crab.

My daughter Jvana also loves to fish and eat seafood. Every summer we would go camping and fishing on the Fraser River.

Jvana had her own way of catching fish. She tied her own lures, cast her line, and when she got a bite, she would turn and run up the beach, dragging the fish behind her.

She was often very successful, and once offered to help other fishermen who seemed to be having trouble catching anything. She was always thoughtful that way!

Norm's Seafood in a Bun

Ingredients

1 lb of assorted cooked seafood - prawns, shrimp, crab, scallops.

1/2 cup of cream cheese

1 pack of frozen spinach - defrost and drain well

Tbsp of parmesan cheese

1/2 cup of asiago cheese

1 minced garlic clove

Juice of 1/2 lemon

4 large bread buns.

Hollow out the buns, so there is a large cavity and discard the bread. Mix all the other ingredients together, except the asiago cheese, and fill the bun cavities with this mixture.

Sprinkle the asiago cheese over each bun.

Bake the filled buns in the oven at 350 degrees for 25 minutes or until the cheese is bubbling and browning.

Crab Cakes

Crab Cakes

Ingredients

1 lb of cooked crab meat

2 tbsps of mayo

2 carrots grated

2 shallots, finely diced

1/2 tsp of garlic powder

1/4 tsp of dill

1 cup of panko seasoned to taste

3 egg yolks, beaten

Canola oil for frying.

Mix all the ingredients, except the panko and egg yolks. Chill overnight or until the mixture has firmed up.

Spoon out a tablespoon of the mixture at a time and form into patties and place on a cookie sheet. Put the cookie sheet of patties into a freezer for at least half an hour so the patties are almost frozen.

Dip each patties firstly into the beaten egg, and then coat evenly with the seasoned panko. Heat the canola oil in a large frying pan and fry each patty on both sides until golden brown.

Serve with Spicy Tomato Relish - see next recipe.

Spicy Tomato Relish

Ingredients

1 cup of sun dried tomatoes (not in oil)

8 cups of fresh tomatoes (halved)

1 tbsp of coriander seed 1

tbsp of mustard seeds 4 garlic cloves

4 red chilli peppers halved (with seeds left in)

4 large onions quartered

2 large red pepper, cut into chunks (without the seeds)

1 cup of brown sugar

3 cups of cider vinegar.

Soak sun dried tomatoes in hot water for 20 minutes. Then drain and add to a food processor with the fresh tomatoes, garlic, onions, chilli peppers and red peppers, and process for 2 minutes.

In a frying pan, dry roast the coriander and mustard seeds over a medium heat for 2 mins, and then crush them.

Add the blended tomato mixture, plus the crushed seeds to a large stock pot, and add the sugar, cider vinegar and a tsp of salt.

Bring to a simmer, and allow to cook for approximately 3 - 4 hours, stirring occasionally to stop the mixture from sticking.

The relish is ready when all the liquid is absorbed. A good check is to use a wooden spoon to make a trail across the top of the mixture - if it fills with liquid, keep simmering, if not, it's ready.

Leave to cool, then fill sterilized jars. Place the jars in a canner, and can for 15 minutes on pressure 5.

Store in a dark place. This relish gets better with age.

Layered Crab Dip

Ingredients

1 lb of cooked crab meat

1/4 cup of sour cream

1/4 cup of mayo

1 Chipotle pepper, finely chopped

3 large fresh tomatoes, diced

2 shallots, finely chopped

2 tbsps fresh cilantro

Salt and pepper to taste.

Mix the sour cream, mayo and chipotle pepper together.

In a shallow glass dish, arrange the crab meat at the bottom. Spread the cream and mayo mixture on top .

Combine the chopped tomatoes, shallots, cilantro and salt and pepper, and add this as the third layer on top the crab and mayo mixture.•

Serve with Nacho chips - just scoop it up.

Mushroom Seafood Caps

Mushroom Seafood Caps

This is a flexible recipe - use small mushrooms for appetizers, or large mushrooms for a main meal. Also the big secret is the teaspoon of melted butter over each cap just before baking....butter makes everything better!

Ingredients

2 lbs of mushrooms

½ lb of shrimp, peeled and cooked (this is usually how you buy it)

1/2 lb of fresh cooked crab meat

3/4 cup of cream cheese

1/2 tsp crushed garlic

1/4 tsp dried dill

1/4 cup of parmesan cheese

1/2 cup of melted butter

Splash of lemon juice

Combine all the seafood with the cream cheese, garlic and dill and chill overnight in the fridge.

Clean and de-stalk the mushrooms and lay out on a greased cookie sheet.

Fill each mushroom cap with a generous dollop of the chilled seafood mixture.

Sprinkle each cap with parmesan cheese and a teaspoon of melted butter.

Bake in the oven at 350 degrees for 15 minutes, and then place under a hot grill for 2 or 3 minutes until golden brown. Serve hot.

Prawn Fishing with Uncle Muck

Uncle "Muck" (Clarence) fished with me for years, and finally retired from commercial fishing a few years after I sold my boat.

These days he has his own boat, the Pacific Skipper and he regularly throws a few prawn traps in the ocean. He won't tell you where all his good "honey holes" though, but he might give you a bag of prawns if you ask nicely.

Until recently, his best friend Tom Cathers was his deckhand. Sadly Tom passed away, but Uncle Muck still gets out there, accompanied by his little dog Freddie.

BC Spot prawns are sweet and tender, and have a massive market in Pacific Asia because they are perfect for sushi.

My favourite way to eat them is straight out of the ocean, blanched in a little sea water, standing on the deck of the Pacific Skipper in the sun.

Grilled Prawns

Ingredients

2 lbs of BC Spot prawn tails, raw and peeled

3/4 lb of butter, melted 3 shallots, finely chopped

4 cloves of garlic, crushed

Juice of 1/2 lemon

2 tbsp of chopped parsley

1/2 cup of breadcrumbs

1 egg yolk

2 tsps of hot sauce

Salt and pepper to taste.

Rinse and pat dry the prawn tails. Place them in a large flat pan. Mix the butter, shallots, garlic, lemon juice, parsley, bread crumbs, egg yolk, hot sauce and seasoning together.

Spoon the mixture over the raw prawns and place under a grill for 3 to 5 minutes, turning the prawns so they do not overcook.

Serve the prawns with warm bread to mop up the excess butter mixture.

Prawn Cocktail

This recipe is so simple, it's embarrassing. But it looks awesome and tastes spectacular.

To blanch the prawns, plunge raw unpeeled prawn tails into boiling water for about three minutes

Ingredients

1 lb of BC Spot prawns, peeled and blanched

2 Tbsps of ketchup

1 Tbsp of Hot Horseradish Sauce

Dash of hot sauce

Chopped parsley

Lemon Wedges

Mix together the ketchup , horseradish sauce and hot sauce. Coat the blanched peeled prawns in the mixture and serve in small dishes (or clam shells, as shown) and garnish with a sprinkle of parsley and lemon wedges.

Prawn Risotto

Ingredients

6 - 7 cups of chicken stock

3 tbsps olive oil

1 large onion, finely chopped

3 stalks of celery, finely chopped

2 garlic cloves, crushed

1 cup of Arborio rice

1/2 cup of dry white wine

3 cups of fresh peeled prawn tails

1 tbsp of butter

Salt and pepper to season.

Heat the stock in a large saucepan, just keep it on a low heat, barely simmering. In a frying pan heat the olive oil and add the onion, celery and garlic. Saute slowly on a medium heat until the veg is soft.

Turn up the heat, and add the dry rice and stir until the rice starts to fry and turns translucent - do not let the rice go brown. Add the cup of wine and stir until the rice absorbs the wine. Turn down the heat to medium.

Add a ladle of warm stock from the saucepan and stir until absorbed by the rice. Repeat and repeat again, until the rice is soft and starts to get a little starchy.

This process may take up to half an hour.

Add the prawns to the rice mixture, and stir until the prawns are cooked through, they will lose their translucent look.

Remove from heat, add the butter and seasoning and stir well.

Allow to sit for two mins before serving.

Prawn Curry

Ingredients

1 lb of raw peeled prawns

1 medium red onion

1 small chunk of fresh ginger peeled

3 garlic cloves

2 stalks of celery, chopped

Small head of cauliflower - remove stalk and divide into small florets

2 fresh tomatoes - chopped

Chopped fresh cilantro (garnish)

Spice. Mix

2 tsp of garam masala

1 tsp of turmeric

1 tsp of cumin

1 tsp of ground coriander

1 tsp of cayenne pepper

1 tsp of cinnamon

1/2 tsp of nutmeg

Pinch of salt and pepper

Prawn Curry (cont)

Combine the spices in a small bowl.

Combine the onion, ginger and garlic in a food processor and blend into a paste.

Heat the olive oil in a large pan, and add the paste mixture. Cook until the paste begins to 'sweat'.

Add the celery, cauliflower and tomatoes, and cook until veg is soft, adding the chicken stock as needed to stop the mixture sticking. As the veg cooks, add the spice mixture.

Once the veg is cooked, add the raw prawns and cook until the prawns are no longer translucent, about five minutes.

Add the coconut milk, and stir thoroughly.

Serve hot over basmati or jasmine rice, and sprinkle with the fresh cilantro.

Scallops, Mussels, Clams & Oyster

Saltspring Mussels In White Wine & Garlic

Ingredients

5 lbs of Saltspring Mussels, cleaned and "de-bearded"

1 large white onion, diced

3 cloves of garlic, crushed

1/2 cup of butter

1/2 cup of olive oil

1 bottle of dry white wine

1 tbsp of chopped parsley.

Saltspring Island is situated off the East Coast of Vancouver Island. It's famous for the weekly Farmer's Market and the artisans that live and work there. And all the hippies. And of course, the flavourful Mussels that grow around the coastline.

Melt the butter in a large stock pot with the olive oil. Saute the onion until soft. Add the chopped parsley, garlic and white wine, and then add the cleaned mussels.

Cook / steam the mussels in the covered stock pot, until the mussels shells have opened.

Serve the mussels with a generous helping of the white wine juice, this can be mopped up with French bread.

Note - discard any mussels that do not open during cooking.

Broiled Ginger Scallops (Tony Elliott)

Ingredients

1 lb Scallops

1/4 cup Soy Sauce

1/4 cup Lemon Juice

2 Tbsp Olive Oil

2 Tbsp Chopped Ginger Root

1 Tbsp Honey

If Scallops are larger, cut them into halves. Arrange the scallops in a single layer baking dish.

Heat the soy sauce to boiling point. Add the finely chopped ginger root, and reduce the heat. Simmer uncovered for 5 minutes.

Stir in the rest of the ingredients and pour over the scallops. Cover and place in the fridge for two hours.

Set the oven to broil. Take the scallops out of the marinade and place on a broiling rack. Cook for five minutes.

Makes enough for three people. Or just one person, if you don't want to share.

Pan Seared Scallops with Mint Pesto

Ingredients

1 lb of scallops (approx. 12)

1/2 cup of butter

Tbsp of olive oil.

Juice of half a lemon.

For Mint Pesto

4 cups of fresh mint leaves

½ cup of unsalted pistachio nuts (shelled and peeled)

2 large cloves of garlic

1/4 cup of olive oil.

Puree all the Mint Pesto ingredients in a blender, and add a touch more olive oil to serve.

Heat up the butter and oil in a pan, until it is very hot. Place the scallops around the pan, clockwise (so you know which scallop to turn first). Sear for a minute or a minute and half each side, until they lose their transparent look.

Serve with a sprinkle of salt and pepper and a drizzle of Mint Pesto.

Digging Clams

Clam Digging was a family affair for us. It was a way to earn extra money throughout the year as well as a food source.

When I was about five years old, the whole family went camping for the summer at Rebecca Spit on Quadra Island.

I think Dad was beach combing, we were clam digging, and picking berries... we were just running free, and having a blast.

My mom often tells the story of my first entrepreneurial endeavour.

A group of Americans had moored their boat just off the Spit, and were exploring the beach.

They had seen us digging clams, and were trying to do the same, but with little success. I grabbed my clam digger and went over to them and as soon showing them how to dig.

This big American said "How much for the bucket of clams?" Without hesitating, I said 'Five bucks".

My mom heard this exchange, and was horrified..... "Bob!! Give them the clams!!"

"Now now mother" the American said,

"This young gentleman and I are in the middle of a business transaction".

I got my five bucks and the American's got their clams.

Clam Fritters

Ingredients

1 cup of All Purpose flour

1 tsp baking powder

1/4 tsp salt

1/ 4 tsp pepper

1 can of minced clams

1 egg

3 Tbsp of milk

1/2 cup of finely diced onion

1 small can of creamed corn.

Canola oil for frying

Lemon wedges.

Mix the dry ingredients together in a bowl. In a separate bowl, beat the egg together with the milk. Add the egg mixture to the dry ingredients, along with the can of clams, and can of creamed corn and diced onion.

Mix thoroughly until it is a batter consistency.

Heat the canola oil in a pan until it is very hot - should even start smoking a little. Drop large tablespoons of the clam batter into the oil and fry until golden brown.

Serve with a lemon wedges.

Seafood Chowder

Ingredients

6 rashers of smoked bacon, cubed

1 lb of small potatoes, cubed

6 small carrots, diced

2 cans of creamed corn

1 onion, diced small

1 large can of clams

2 litres of chicken stock

3 lbs of fresh seafood - shrimp, prawns, halibut (dice large pieces of fish into bite size cubes)

Small carton of light cream

1/4 cup of olive oil

Fry the bacon and onion in the olive oil until the onion is translucent. Add the diced vegetable, creamed corn, canned clams and chicken stock. Bring to the boil and then simmer for approximately 2 hours. Add all the seafood and the light cream and simmer for a further 15 minutes. Season to your taste and serve immediately.

This recipe will make enough chowder for ten servings. If you prefer, you can freeze the soup, before you add the seafood and cream. However, the leftovers the next day are even better, because the seafood flavours have really had time to marinate. This chowder is excellent served with Bannock.

Bannock

Ingredients

3 cups of All Purpose flour

2 tbsp baking powder

1 tsp salt

1/4 cup of olive oil

1 1/2 cups of water.

Mix all the dry ingredients together in a large bowl.

Add the olive oil and mix well.

Gradually add the water, mixing all the time until a smooth dough is formed Turn out the dough onto a floured surface, and roll out until the dough is an inch thick and then cut into 12 squares.

Bake in a pre-heated oven, 350 degrees for 25 minutes or until the bannock is golden brown.

Serve warm.

Seafood Salad (Daniel Elliott)

Ingredients

1 lb of prawns, peeled and broiled (or peeled cooked shrimp, or scallops or all of them!)

1 can of black beans (drained and rinsed)

1 can of sweets corn (drained)

1 pineapple - peeled and cubed

1 Mango, peeled and cubed

Handful of fresh chopped cilantro

Dressing

4 Tbsp of olive oil

Juice of 3 Limes

Tsp of cumin

Combine and toss all the ingredients in one bowl and serve chilled.

Easy!

Seafood & Black Bean Pasta

Ingredients

1 lb of fresh seafood - prawns, shrimp or scallops

Couple of handfuls of your favourite dried pasta

6 tbsp of olive oil

3 garlic cloves, crushed

2 small red chilli peppers, chopped finely

3 tbsp of Black Bean paste (not sauce, the paste has a more intense flavour)

Cook the pasta according to instructions, drain well and toss in a little olive oil.

In a shallow frying pan or wok, heat up the olive oil and add the garlic and chilli peppers, and saute for about five minutes.

Just as the garlic starts to turn colour, add the black bean paste and stir thoroughly to heat through.

Add the seafood and cook for another five minutes, or until it is cooked through. Add the cooked pasta to the wok and toss all the ingredients together, and serve hot.

Pan Fried Oysters

Ingredients

1 quart of medium sized shucked oysters (about 20)

1 tbsp of garlic powder 1/ 4 cup of soy sauce

1/ 4 cup of light teriyaki sauce.

For the coating

2 egg yolks

1/4 cup of light cream

1/ 2 cup of panko

1/ 2 tsp of dill

Salt and pepper to season.

Canola oil for frying

In a large saucepan of water, bring the oysters, garlic powder, soy sauce and teriyaki to a boil, and then reduce to a simmer for five minutes.

Drain the oysters and pat dry.

Beat the egg yolk together with the cream, and mix the panko with the seasonings. Dip the oysters first into the egg mixture, then coat evenly with the panko mix.

Heat the canola oil in a shallow frying pan, and fry the coated oysters until golden brown all over.

Smoked and Canned Oysters

Oysters are farmed all around Vancouver Island. It is possible to pick them yourself, but it's much safer to purchase them from an oyster farm. Sadly, due to pollution, much of the coast experiences "Red Tide" with is a high level of algae in the seawater. It doesn't kill the oysters, but it will kill humans.

I always boil oysters before cooking, to get rid of the fishy smell. I use the same ingredients as Pan Fried Oysters - see previous recipe.

I place the oysters on a rack in my smoke house after boiling them. Again, if you have a smoker such as a Little Chief, it's exactly the same procedure.

Smoke the oyster for approximately eight hours until they brown up and are firm - almost feel rubbery to the touch.

They would be great just like this, but I go one step further and can them in olive oil.

Place the smoked oysters in cans or small mason jars and fill up with good quality olive oil.

Can them in a pressure cooker for 100 minutes at 10 lbs pressure.

When they have cooled down, check that each one has sealed properly. These oyster are spectacular on a cracker or bread with cream cheese.

The Silver Eagle

After years of fishing and running other people's boat, I wanted my own. I briefly experienced being the owner / skipper back when I had the Skeeter II, and now being older and hopefully wiser, I wanted my own Seine boat.

She wasn't pretty, and she needed a lot of work. She was a repo. She was originally named the Leader III. She needed a new motor, hydraulics, a deck winch, new wiring and, oh yes, a net.

I started working on her in the December of 1985, kept on working on her until the day I went fishing the next June and kept on working on her until the day I sold her. There was no one part of the boat, except the hull, that I didn't work on, repair or replace. The boat came with a seine licence.

I renamed the boat "Silver Eagle" ahnost immediately and was amazed that the name wasn't already registered on another.

I fished for J .S McMillan Fisheries, based in Vancouver. The first year fishing for them with the Silver Eagle, I was 54th out of 55 boats. The 55th had been in the shipyard all season. I had been broke down more time than I had been fishing, and consequently I earned $2500.

It was a heavy responsibility, because I not only had crew who wanted to earn a living, I also had boat payments to make.

Barry McMillan, one of the owners I fished for, called me into the office and said "Bob, whatever you are doing out there, it isn't working. You need to improve". No kidding.

So I put my head down and kept going. After one particularly bad day, after being towed in to Port McNeil with a seized engine, I was tied to the dock and feeling pretty sorry for myself.

It was there that I met Billy Richards, who would be my deckhand until I sold the boat. He was completely haywire, but my best deckhand, with the exception of my Uncle "Muck" Clarence who was my boat engineer for years too.

We finally got the boat working that day and went out fishing. Billy was a total greenhorn, but I told him to do exactly what I said, and he did.

That day we caught seven or eight thousand sockeye. It was the turning point for the Silver Eagle, we made some money, but more importantly, my self-confidence came back.

Every year after that it got better and better. Finally in 1992, the Silver Eagle was high boat. That means I caught more fish than any other in the J.S McMillan Fleet. My friend Johnny Millicheap and his boat "The Lasqueti Storm" was also top of the heap that year for Bella Coo la Fisheries.

He got a free trip to Hawaii. I got a nice letter. I didn't care, my little aluminum falling apart old boat had caught more fish than most of the million dollar boats on the BC Coast. I fished through some of the golden years of salmon fishing. But all good things come to an end.

In the mid nineties, the Department of Fisheries announced a "buy back". That meant they would purchase back fishing licences, in order to reduce the fishing fleet. They promised that the remaining West Coast fleet would benefit from better fishing. It wasn't true.

I took the buy back and sold my boat privately. It was the end of my fishing career, and shortly after that, the end of the Silver Eagle's fishing days too.

For the majority of those golden days, my main crew were Billy Richards, Buffalo Bill, Uncle Muck, my cousin Glen Elliott and my two little galley slaves, Norman and Jason.

www.ingramcontent.com/pod-product-compliance
Lightning Source LLC
Chambersburg PA
CBHW051552010526
44118CB00022B/2679